Contents

Using This Guide

BACKGROUND OF STUDY

The Old Testament is law; the New Testament is grace. That misconception has plagued the church and Christian theology, not to mention Jewish-Christian relationships, for almost two millennia. The truth of the matter is that grace weaves its way throughout the Hebrew Scriptures, often coming to the fore at critical junctures. Nowhere is that revelation clearer in the Hebrew Scriptures than in Genesis. This book of "beginnings" (as Genesis and its Hebrew parallel *beresit* literally mean) declares God's disposition toward humanity and creation to be a fundamentally gracious one. That is, God consistently does for us what we cannot do for ourselves and what we have done nothing to merit.

Set in the reflective time of Lent, this study will explore the dynamics of God's grace. The narratives of Genesis and the spiritual journeys of its characters will provide the starting points; but at its heart, this study intends to discern the movement of grace among and within the lives of persons today. Thus, the lives of those participating in these sessions—and your own—provide the parallel "texts" to Genesis.

SESSION COMPONENTS

Each session will contain the following elements:
- Overview
- Preparing for the Session
- Leading the Session
- Review / Preview

The Overview will outline the session's main themes and any contemporary issues the material may raise for participants.

Consideration of the overview may enable you to discern themes and issues of special interest to your group.

Preparing for the Session will identify resources to procure or arrangements to make prior to the session itself.

Leading the Session provides the actual plan of basic and alternate experiences for each session. The session plans themselves follow a threefold understanding of grace: grace *calls*, grace *forms*, and grace *commissions*.

- *Grace calls us into community:* The first movement of the session involves recognition of God's presence through worship and the gathering of the community around the session's themes.

- *Grace forms us by word and experience:* The second movement of the session entails encounter with the Genesis material and then a connection with our own spiritual journeys.

- *Grace commissions us to serve and trust:* The third movement of the session explores avenues of embodying grace and celebrating the God to whom we entrust our lives.

Review / Preview encourages reflection on the session just completed and the incorporation of those learnings into future sessions.

ENCOUNTERING THE TEXT

Each session builds upon the previous week's readings from Genesis. Time constraints probably will not allow a reading of *all* those texts within the session. However, for purposes of review and/or fresh hearing (for members unable to do all the readings or for visitors who did none), *some* of the stories lend themselves to oral presentation in the session.

Each session will list several suggested focus readings. Consider when and how you might involve the readings in the session.

When. One of two times seems most appropriate:

- at the outset of the "Grace Calls Us" section (after greeting all). The reading would set the tone for all that follows.
- at the beginning of the "Grace Forms Us" section.

Consider which placement would most help the participants, while enhancing the flow of the session.

How. Be flexible. Options might include:

- Designate one person to read the texts aloud.
- Spread the readings among several persons (always check beforehand participants' comfort level with reading aloud). Consider having each reader take the role of a particular character or serve as the narrator.
- Involve a storyteller to summarize the text's stories in a single narrative.
- Think about using prerecorded audiotapes of the sessions' readings or videotape a dramatic retelling of the texts.

Be open to varying your method from week to week depending on the types of experiences and activities each session requires. Whenever and however the reading takes place, allow time and opportunity to (re)encounter the Genesis stories.

WORSHIP CENTER

Worship is meant to be an integral part of each session. A study of grace is a study of divine encounter—which means, among other things, that it brings us to stand on holy ground. A purely academic study might be able to avoid a devotional component, but this is not such a study. Grace seeks out head and heart, mind and will: a seeking not fully acknowledged if devoid of the sense and act of worship.

Whether in rainbows arched across the sky or stones piled into an altar or a ladder ascending into heaven, Genesis provides a variety of visual images for the meaning of encounter with God's grace. Likewise, the session guides suggest using visible symbols as part of each gathering to create worship centers. If others in the group (or you) wonder if people find such visual aids to worship helpful, think about the sanctuary in which you and the group members worship. Windows, crosses, flowers, table and/or altar, ceiling design, colors: How many of these or other symbols form the backdrop for your experience of liturgy?

The worship center simply attempts to provide a focused experience of "sanctuary" (sacred space) in each session. Don't hesitate to improvise on these suggestions for worship centers. Make the weekly "sanctuary" as appropriate to your group as possible. On a broader note, keep the same idea in mind with the entire leader's guide. It is only a guide; use it creatively.

ALTERNATE ACTIVITIES

Some groups thrive on discussion; some need experiential activities. Some groups have access to a variety of resources and materials; some groups have limited access. A host of factors plays into these and other differences in group dynamics. No single leader's guide will provide the perfect resource for each and every group that wishes to use it.

However, the suggested alternate activities for each session offer one way of addressing such variances. For the most part, the alternate activities involve either more materials or experiential projects. The basic session involves an hour of time and requires somewhat limited resources. Groups with more time and greater access to resources may choose to do both the basic and alternate activities—or some combination.

Again, when using this guide, be creative. Use the suggested activities and experiences that best suit your group. Modify them as needed or fashion your own activities.

LEADER AS PARTICIPANT

Genesis of Grace is a book of daily readings and reflections for the season of Lent. This leader's guide offers one possible way for a group to study this resource in weekly gatherings. Fundamental to such a study, however, is maintaining the discipline of reading daily. Time for conscious reflection on the reading over the course of each day will help build a sense of continuity and movement. Setting aside time for the daily reflections upon God's grace at work in the characters of Genesis will create greater opportunity to consider God's grace at work in the lives of the participants.

Encourage the participants to adhere to this daily "vigil"— and keep it yourself. With sessions to prepare, you may well find it necessary to "look ahead" at the week's later readings to gain perspective on the session's themes and suggested experiences. Even so, do not neglect the designated reading and reflective time each day. Your best preparation for this study will take place in that daily discipline. Enjoy the opportunity to be a participant yourself in this exploration of grace. Seek the leading of the Spirit in your reflection. Then lead the sessions from that shared experience.

Week One: Dust and Seeds

Focus Readings: 2:7, 18, 21-22; 3:8-13; 4:3-10, 13-15

OVERVIEW

The beginning stories of grace in Genesis touch on a surprising complexity of issues. The paradox of human origins in the humility of dust as well as the very breath of God, loneliness and community, the flight from responsibility through blaming others, jealousy, justice counterpoised to mercy: All are bound by the constant presence of a tenaciously gracious God.

What issues receive a "high profile" in your community or church at the moment? Racial prejudice might find an interesting counterpoint in the story of God's fashioning *'adam* (Adam) from *'adamah* (pedigrees of purity dissolve in common clay). Those who demand a punitive criminal justice system might find God's dealing with Cain a troublesome bit of coddling.

PREPARING FOR THE SESSION

Read the stories and devotional reflections as if written to your church and community. What might your study group find most affirming, most unsettling? Why? Set aside extra time in the session for such issues if you feel it will enhance the participants' experience of these texts and God's grace.

Resources Needed

- (worship center) Large pot or planter filled with potting soil, bowl or large cup with flower seeds (you might consult a gardener about flowers that grow well in your area)
- Words and music to "Hymn of Promise" or another song or chorus about grace (musical accompaniment would be appropriate)
- Chalkboard and chalk *or* newsprint and markers

- Wet washcloths and dry towels to clean hands after planting seeds

LEADING THE SESSION

Grace Calls Us

- Greet each person by name. Introduce persons who may not be known to everyone.
- Offer a prayer of invocation (one of your own composition or the following): *Holy God, whose hands have shaped us from the dust, whose breath has filled us with life, whose Spirit surrounds us with grace: Move and work among us anew that we may see our promise, acknowledge our failings, and render our service as those stamped with your image. In Jesus Christ. Amen.*
- Sing a song or chorus that celebrates the gift of grace seen in creation. One suggestion would be "Hymn of Promise" by Natalie Sleeth. If the tune is unfamiliar, the group may sing the words to the tune of "Joyful, Joyful, We Adore Thee" (Beethoven's "Hymn to Joy"). Spend a few moments afterward discussing how this song (or the one you chose) depicts or envisions God's grace.
- On a chalkboard or newsprint sheet, record participants' responses that would complete the line: "Grace is...." Encourage as many associations with grace as possible.

ALTERNATE EXPERIENCE   In pairs, have participants share earliest or most decisive recollections of God's grace in their lives. What was "gracious" about those events? How have those experiences influenced their faith and living?

- Call attention to the pot or planter with dirt and to the bowl with seeds on the worship center. Cup each of your hands with some of the dirt and seeds, letting them pour down into their respective containers so everyone can see. Ask what connection the "grace phrases" recorded earlier might have with these common things of the earth. Lead the discussion to what dust and seeds have to do with this week's readings from Genesis. Such ideas might include the following: human creation from dust, return to dust at death, Eve's "seed" as hope's promise, Cain's sowing the seed of tragedy and the crying out of the ground (dust) in return.

Grace Forms Us

- Invite participants to identify characters encountered in this week's readings. Ask, "What type of soil or seed would you associate with the characters based on their words and actions? Why?" Discuss what we would know of grace if a character's story were our only source of knowledge about it.

ALTERNATE EXPERIENCE Form four small groups and assign each group a character from this week's readings: Adam, Eve, Cain, Abel. Have each cluster prepare a presentation to the larger group on its character's experience of grace. Address how grace changed that character, as well as its effects on his or her relationships with others and God. Afterward, encourage interaction among the "characters" by asking clusters to respond to one another's assertions.

- Move either of the above discussions from the varied roles grace played in these characters' lives to the lives of persons today. For example, ask adults to indicate with which character's experience of grace they most identify, and why.

- In groups of three or four persons, explore the actions that threaten grace in these texts: hiding, casting blame on others, resentment. How do participants see these same stories played out in their own lives and relationships? (You might remind them of Jesus' teaching in the Sermon on the Mount in Matthew 5:21-22, where the demeaning of brother or sister serves as an equivalent to murder). How does grace seek to mend such breaches: in the stories of Genesis, in contemporary (and personal) experiences?

- Invite participants to raise questions or issues suggested by the previous week's readings. For example, discuss how demands for a punitive justice system might judge God's granting of sanctuary to the murderer Cain. Address concerns as best you can based on your own wrestling with these issues as well as the experience of others in the group. Understand that not all issues will have answers, even as the text does not answer all the questions it raises.

Grace Commissions Us

- Ask group members silently to consider the "communities" of which they are a part: family, church, friendships, business, clubs, school, etc. Say, "Imagine the particular faces and lives of those who comprise those communities. (*pause for a time of silence and reflection*) Reflect on how those communities have 'graced' your life, how they have been instruments of God's working in your life."
- Have members find a partner, ideally someone they trust. Ask partners to share with each other some of those ways in which community has been a vehicle of grace in their lives.

ALTERNATE EXPERIENCE Call the group together. Based on conversations with partners, discuss ways in which your church community might better serve as a vehicle of grace for others. Be specific. Record responses on newsprint. Briefly identify leaders or groups in the church with whom a member might share these ideas.

- Gather the group at the worship center. Confirm that just as we have to plant seeds for seeds to achieve their potential, we also have to use the grace God brings to our lives.

Recall the characters in this week's readings: What difference did grace make in their lives?

- Move the discussion from the characters to the lives of persons gathered about this worship center. Invite group members to suggest ways these stories relate to their own spiritual journeys. As with the characters, how has grace made a difference in the lives of the group members? Be specific.
- Give each person one or more seeds. Ask members to consider the seeds as symbols of the grace extended to us in our creation. As the group sings the song used earlier, have participants dig in the soil and plant their seeds as an act of trust in and commitment to God's grace. Assign one person the responsibility of caring for the pot or planter. If taken home between sessions, ask that it be returned each week so that class members may observe the growth (let's hope!).
- Close with a sentence prayer, in which each member may offer thanks for the gift and promise of God's grace.

REVIEW / PREVIEW

Make note of those activities/elements that went well and those that did not. Plan future sessions accordingly. Also identify discussions that went unfinished or unresolved and might benefit from further conversation in future sessions.

The Noah stories broaden the context of Genesis back to its starting point, which is the entire creation, in judgment (6:7) and covenant (9:9-10). At the same time, they bring the setting of grace into its tightest focus, which is the heart of both human and divine. The question looms: Will sin in the human heart overwhelm the grace toward creation that resides in God's heart?

Week Two: Matters of the Heart

Focus Readings: 6:5-8; 7:6-12; 8:1, 8-12, 20-22; 9:8-11

OVERVIEW

How does God deal with evil? How wide a circle does God embrace with covenant? Can our actions reach into the heart of God? The Noah stories raise big questions about the role of grace in a world that has not lived up to its potential.

Contemporary issues raised by these texts vary widely. As we approach the year 2000, prediction of end-time disaster scenarios will increase. How does God's covenanted "Never again" address theologies that seem to relish the pronouncement of destruction as the precursor to glory? In a different vein, deliverance for those borne up by the ark comes in the act of God's remembrance. How do we communicate saving remembrance to those whom illness, oppression, and economies stigmatize as the forgotten of our time: whether they be Alzheimer patients or political prisoners or sub-Saharan refugees?

PREPARING FOR THE SESSION

As you explore the texts and their devotional meditations, what do you think the members of your study group will hear in them? What matters of their hearts will come to the forefront? Couple those anticipations with the session's suggested plans as you prepare to lead this week's study. Let the words of the text address your heart with the word and challenge of grace.

Resources Needed

- (worship center) Globe or picture of the earth from space
- Magazines (pictorial more than text), scissors, paste or glue
- Two large sheets of newsprint or poster board, each cut in heart shape

- (alternate experience) Check with your local Public Broadcasting Station or public library for the video *The Mind* (Part 1, "The Search for Mind"), VCR, television
- Newsprint and markers *or* chalkboard and chalk
- Precut paper hearts (at least one per member), pens

LEADING THE SESSION

Grace Calls Us

- Greet persons by name. Welcome newcomers or visitors and introduce them to others in the group.
- Give instructions to make two collages on the heart-shaped newsprint or poster board: one for the heart of God, one for the human heart. Instruct members to imagine they can see into both hearts. Cut or tear out pictures and images that symbolize what persons would see in each. Do the collages.
- When completed, display both collages where all may see them. Elicit responses on what the finished collages convey in the way of meaning or feeling—this is *not* a time for persons to say what they added and why. If desired, let participants make such comments after sharing reactions and impressions.

ALTERNATE EXPERIENCE Focus on the similarities and differences between the two collages. Where is our creation in the image of God still evident in the collage of the human heart? Where negative images or pictures appear on that collage, discuss options by which the human heart could be "cleansed." What would be the results? the risks?

- Offer the following prayer of invocation or another of your own creation: *Loving God, you open your heart to us in creation and in love. Be present with us now. Open our hearts to your Spirit, open our minds to your leading. Remind us not only of our fashioning in your image but of our calling to your service. In Jesus Christ. Amen.*

Grace Forms Us

- Ask members to suggest ways in which these collages might have differed had the members used only Genesis 6–9 as the basis of their imagery. What would they have added to the collages? What would they have deleted? Why? What statements and inferences about the heart, both human and divine, do members hear from the passages this past week?

- Form two groups. Announce that one group is to be a prosecution team, the other a defense team. The case being contested is this: Should God repeat the Flood (or some similar disaster) to remove evil from the world? The prosecution will argue for; the defense will argue against. Both sides are to develop reasons for their position and risks inherent in their opposition's position. Allow time to caucus and decide on strategy. Then allow each side to present its case, followed by an opportunity to rebut each other's arguments. Encourage appeals to Genesis 6–9 and to the collages. After the exercise, review the debate. What makes us prone to seek justice or to offer mercy? Why?

- Have members find a partner. Review Clive's story from the PBS documentary (Sunday's reading). Ask members to put themselves in Clive's place. Discuss from that perspective: What remembrances would you miss most? How could you experience hope? What would a collage of the heart without remembrance look like?

ALTERNATE EXPERIENCE View segment 1, "The Search for Mind," of the PBS/BBC-produced documentary *The Mind** that features Clive's life and affliction. After viewing, invite responses from members to what they have seen. Next discuss the role of remembrance in Clive's life, in their own lives, in this week's texts from Genesis. What does remembrance make possible? How are remembrance and grace interrelated? (*A production of WNET, New York and the BBC [British Broadcasting Corporation] © 1988 by Public Educational Service. Check your public library or video rental store.)

- In groups of three or four, read Genesis 9:8-17 aloud. Identify the elements of this first biblical covenant: the parties involved; the promises offered. Give time for discussion, then return to the large group. Ask, "If this were the only covenant in Genesis, what would it reveal to us about God, about the world, about you and me?" Allow for conversation. Discuss how this covenant conveys God's grace through its choice of parties as well as its promises. In what ways do members identify with this covenant today?

Grace Commissions Us

- Prepare four sheets of newsprint or divide one sheet into fourths. Write one of these titles on each sheet or section: *Mission, Worship, Education, Evangelism.* Ask members to identify ways and actions in which the church testifies to a God who graces life with saving remembrance and covenant; that is, what do we do in mission or worship or education or evangelism that reveals a God who remembers and covenants? Examples might include mission (*we feed and shelter persons whom others sometimes forget*), worship (*we hear the old stories read and interpreted for today's living*), education (*we study the covenants in order to live by their conditions and promises*), evangelism (*we bring God's good news to those inside and outside our circles*).

Give each person at least one small cutout heart. Invite participants to think in silence of a person who might feel forgotten. Say, "Write the first name of that person on one side. On the other side, write a message you think might help the person in this time." Allow time for reflection and writing. Challenge each participant to follow through with this person during the week with a card, a phone call, a visit (ideal) that conveys the gift of remembrance. State, "Carry the heart in your wallet or purse or place it in a prominent place in your home or office. Every time you notice it, think of this person and offer a brief prayer for him or her."

- Gather at the worship center. Place the collages beside the globe or picture of the earth. Invite members to visualize the relationship between these hearts and this world and how God's grace keeps them joined in hope.
- Lead a closing litany, in which each person has the opportunity to offer a sentence of thanks, concern, or petition. At the end of each prayer, lead the group in the response: "Hear this prayer of the heart, O God." When all have offered prayers, conclude with these words: *Receive our prayers into your heart where grace resides, where remembrance is kept, where love endures for all time and beyond time. In Jesus Christ. Amen.*

REVIEW / PREVIEW

Review the session. Consider what worked, what stumbled, what needs incorporation into or deletion from future sessions.

God's grace concerns matters of the heart—but it does not stop there. When the word of grace comes to Abraham and Sarah, feet begin a journey, mouths break out in laughter, and eyes strain to see how far afield grace will lead from familiar vistas. But before then, Babel recounts the challenge faced—and overturned—when fear attempts to resist grace's journey.

Week Three: Journeys

Focus Readings: 11:1-4, 6-8; 12:1-4; 15:1-6; 18:22-23

OVERVIEW

Beginning with the story of Babel and continuing through the Abraham-Sarah narratives, the dynamic nature of God's grace and our response come to the forefront. The popular theme of faith as a journey traces its roots to these stories. Movement is fundamental here to understanding God's grace: in the scattering of Babel's tower-builders, in the leading of Abraham and Sarah. Grace moves persons away from false securities even as it moves persons toward trusting promises and Promise-Giver.

The parallels one might draw between these texts and our times vary. Individuals and communities of faith are not immune to the temptation of circling the wagons and digging in heels. We reach comfort levels in our fellowship partners and patterns of church life from which we find movement or change difficult at best. It is often far easier to visualize the church as an erected building rather than an evolving mission. Yet even the most established of religious habits came as the result of some person or community's daring to step out in faith, risking movement and change—in other words, embarking on a journey.

PREPARING FOR THE SESSION

Read these stories from Genesis and their accompanying devotional texts with the experiences of your study group members in mind. What journeys led them to this community of faith? Where might they—and you—have trouble with God's word to "go from your country"? Work such issues into the session plan, so that the journey made by grace may address their lives and faith.

Resources Needed

- (worship center) Cross; one road map and one map (printed or hand-drawn) of Israel with routes connecting Bethlehem and Nazareth and Jerusalem highlighted
- (alternate experience) Hymnals with opening song (see below in "Grace Calls Us")
- Sheets of unlined paper, pens or pencils

LEADING THE SESSION

Grace Calls Us

- Greet group members by name. Welcome and introduce any newcomers or visitors.
- Pair each person with a partner (with an odd number, you will need to participate). Assign the following exercise: One person begins by saying, "Faith is a journey because..."— and then the partner completes the sentence.

    The first person repeats the same phrase, and the partner completes it with a different reply. Indicate that this will continue for two minutes, after which you will announce that persons will switch roles and continue for the same amount of time. Stress that the important factor is not that persons take a long time to respond but rather that they reply with the first thing that comes to mind. (Two minutes is a maximum amount of time per person.)
- In the large group, invite summary responses as to why faith is a journey. Persons may share only what they heard, not what they said.

ALTERNATE EXPERIENCE Sing a hymn related to the theme of journey or travel. Suggestions include "My Faith, It Is an Oaken Staff" and "Eternal Father, Strong to Save."

Briefly discuss which imagery in the hymn relates to faith as journey and how God's grace relates to that journey.

- Pray for God's guidance and leading in this session.

Grace Forms Us

- Compare and contrast the journeys made by the people of Babel with that taken by Abraham and Sarah. In what ways does each reveal grace? How do those "revealings" of grace touch home to the experience of persons in the group?

- Give each person a blank sheet of paper and pen or pencil. Call attention to the "road maps" by the worship center. Ask participants how maps aid a traveler. Suggest that each group member create a "map" of her or his journey in faith. The map could include on and off ramps, cloverleafs, straightaways, or other visual indicators of their journey with God. Use road signs and landmarks; keep words at a minimum. Direct their thinking with these or other questions: "When has your faith been stopped or detoured? What kinds of events or experiences 'sped' your trust on its way or confused it? What sights and sounds along the way do you remember as shaping your faith?" Allow adequate time for persons to think and then to draft their maps.

- In small groups, explore the maps together. First, each person shares his or her map with the others, responding to questions or comments from others in the group. Members may divulge only those pieces of the journey they wish to share. Second, invite the groups to draw parallels or connections between the journeys represented on their maps with the journeys of Abraham and Sarah (and the people of Babel). Particular focus issues might include times when persons took too much control, times of laughter and joy, times of fresh identities and new birth.

- Next, ask persons to circle on their maps those places where trust came to the forefront, places where they learned lessons in grace. While still in small groups, invite persons to share how they understood grace to be part of that journey.

ALTERNATE EXPERIENCE Take the group on a "journey" through the church building. Stop at various places that one might associate with experiences of trust or grace: Christian education rooms, fellowship hall, pews, communion table, baptismal font. These "stops" along the way can be of your own and the group's choosing. Invite reflections and stories on the importance of these places in the Christian journey. Encourage participants to remember persons with whom they associate these places: teachers, neighbors, relatives, pastors. How have these persons' lives and stories enriched the faith journey of group members?

- (*If you skip the alternate experience*) Have the small groups regather. Invite personal reflections on how this community of faith has influenced the faith journeys of individuals in the group. How is that influence felt now? In what ways might the participants strengthen or deepen that influence for themselves, for others?

Grace Commissions Us

- Gather around the worship center. Once again call attention to the road maps there, underscoring how Lent proceeds as a journey to the cross. Affirm that journey as one that each of us makes in Christian discipleship. Ask persons to view their own spiritual "maps" in silence. Raise these questions for reflection: "When has the cross come into view? When it has, how has grace sustained you?"

- As a sign of commitment to the journey of faith, explain that persons will now come to the worship center, one by one, to place their individual journey maps by the cross. As each person does so, the group will repeat the following prayer affirmation: "May God's grace sustain ___(name)___ on the journey of faith." Proceed with this activity, making sure each person receives that affirmation.

• Close the session with a benediction that uses the following prayer attributed to Saint Patrick: *May the wisdom of God instruct me; the eye of God watch over me; the ear of God hear me; the word of God give sweetness to my speech; the hand of God defend me; and may I follow the way of God.*

> *Christ be with me, Christ before me,*
> *Christ be after me, Christ within me,*
> *Christ beneath me, Christ above me.*

REVIEW / PREVIEW

Evaluate the session: its discussions, its activities, the response and participation of members. Incorporate learnings into future planning. Follow up with individuals who might have had some difficulty with the session's issues.

Sometimes the journey undertaken by faith does not always lead us to places we would choose, much less places we want to be. The stories of Isaac—as child, as spouse, as parent—reveal how ancient are the struggles to live by faith and how human are the lives even of the children of the promise.

Week Four: The Eye of the Storm

Focus readings: 22:1-2, 7-14; 24:62-67; 25:21-28

OVERVIEW

At times the destinies of Isaac and Rebekah seem caught up in events beyond their control: Isaac's being led by Abraham to Moriah; Rebekah's unknowingly following the script of a servant's prayer for Isaac's would-be wife. Even the fates of the unborn children in Rebekah's womb seem fixed. Yet Isaac and Rebekah find grace: God provides; love unfolds; promises are kept. And Isaac and Rebekah still must make choices, particularly those involving the exercise of parental love.

Bridges exist between the Isaac-Rebekah stories and our own. One fundamental link comes in our identifying with how Isaac and Rebekah conduct their lives in the midst of events beyond their control. Like Abraham, we do not always choose the journeys we make. Sometimes faith takes shape as we discover God's grace along life's unasked-for ways. We may also empathize with Rebekah's cry of, "If it is to be this way, why do I live?" (Gen. 25:22). The struggle of her unborn children evoked her lament. What spurs our protest of "the way things are"? Does that protest lead us to service or despair? Finally, these stories remind us that love either graces life in love's sharing or twists life in love's withholding.

PREPARING FOR THE SESSION

Read the stories and reflections with an empathy for both their characters and the lives of those in your group. Try to anticipate where the points of contact between text and life might be for group members. Let the stories address your own life, so that your leading of this session will evidence an understanding and experience of the text from within.

Resources Needed

- (worship center) Construction paper, newsprint, and/or butcher paper; scissors; markers; tacks or tape to affix the mural
- (alternate experience) Cassette or CD player, recording of storm audio (see suggestions below)
- (alternate experience) Recruit two volunteers to play the roles of Isaac and Rebekah in an "interview."

LEADING THE SESSION

Grace Calls Us

- Welcome the members by name as they enter. Introduce any visitors or guests.
- Instruct members to create a mural of storm clouds that will be placed on or near the worship area. The larger the mural, the better. Indicate that the mural should also depict the "eye" of the storm: a place of calm in the midst of the turbulence. As persons create the mural, invite conversations on persons' experiences of storms, particularly what it feels like to be caught up in the midst of winds and forces beyond one's control.

ALTERNATE EXPERIENCE During the mural-creating activity, provide appropriate audio background. Music selections might include *V, Cloudburst* sequence from Ferde Grofé's *Grand Canyon Suite* or Rimsky-Korsakov's *Night on the Bare Mountain.* You can also find recordings of actual storms on some of the natural sound tapes and CDs.

Instruct participants to share with a partner one or two "storm" experiences in life, times when they found themselves caught up in forces or events beyond their control.

- Offer a prayer of invocation.

Grace Forms Us '

- Invite members to recall this past week's readings on Isaac and Rebekah. Ask, "What were the 'storm' times in Isaac and Rebekah's lives? What made them so? Write the participants' responses on the storm cloud mural. Then discuss parallels and contrasts between crises faced by Isaac and Rebekah and those experienced by group members.
- Consider using one or both of the alternate experiences.

ALTERNATE EXPERIENCE In small groups of three or four, rewrite Genesis 22:1-14 as told from Isaac's perspective. Address these issues (among others): Isaac's relationship to his father, the effect of this experience on Isaac's faith and ability to trust, the meaning of grace for Isaac. Afterward, invite each group to read its rewrite aloud. How do the rewrites speak to our lives, to our times of testing and experiences of grace?

ALTERNATE EXPERIENCE In small groups of three or four, read Genesis 25:22-23 and then compose a diary entry for that day as if written by Rebekah. Focus on her words, "If it is to be this way. . . ." Record her hopes and fears for her children, for the world into which they will be born. Then have each group read its diary entries aloud. How do Rebekah's thoughts address our own wonderings about the ways things are?

- Draw attention to the part of the mural that represents the "eye of the storm." Discuss where and how Isaac and Rebekah experienced grace that sustained them through difficult times.
- Have persons return to the partner with whom they earlier shared their "storm" experiences in life. Invite partners to identify how (and from whom) they found support and strength through those times. In particular, draw the conversation toward the role that faith played in those times and

how and where the participants understood "grace" to have been communicated. In the larger group, summarize those sources and experiences of grace.

ALTERNATE EXPERIENCE Role play an interview with Isaac and Rebekah on the topic of love (see "Preparing for the Session"). Form chairs in a circle around the two volunteers recruited earlier in the week. Inform the group that the topic of this interview is Isaac and Rebekah's love for each other and for their children. They will field questions about their love. To preface the interview, read Genesis 24:67 and 25:28. After the interview, debrief with a discussion on what happens when love—and those who love—play favorites.

• Discuss in small groups the Wednesday devotional reading's portrayal of Isaac as the one who, more than Abraham, experiences the fulfillment of God's promises. With whom do participants identify more? Why? Ask them to share times when they have experienced the fulfillment of promises. How did such fulfillment influence their faith?

Grace Commissions Us

• Gather in the worship area around the storm cloud mural. Review how that visual image has been used through this session to portray times in which we felt ourselves (and saw Isaac and Rebekah) swept along by powerful forces. Next, call to mind that portion of the mural that depicts the eye of the storm. Invite persons to reflect silently on those experiences that brought hope and grace to them in the midst of stress. Ask, "How have those moments of grace stayed with you? How have such moments influenced your actions toward others?"

ALTERNATE EXPERIENCE Offer members the opportunity to write words of thanks to someone whose promise-keeping and love have graced their lives. If those persons are still living, encourage members to send notes or to call and talk to them this week. If the persons are deceased, place the notes by the mural's eye of the storm.

- Join hands in a circle. Allow those persons who wish to do so to offer a prayer of thanks for the way in which God's grace sustained them through one of their "storm" times. If they choose, the prayer may include thanks for persons who conveyed that grace to them. When all have prayed who choose to do so, close by uniting in the Lord's Prayer.

REVIEW / PREVIEW

Within a day following this session, review the activities and discussion. Did members find the mural creation a helpful "hands-on" way to involve themselves in the theme, or do they prefer more cerebral entries into the subject matter? Consider such issues for planning and selecting activities, particularly from the alternate experiences, for the remaining two sessions.

Of all the promise-bearers in Genesis, Jacob is certainly the most questionable. His actions, his deceits, his bargainings with God—all seem to weigh against God's selecting him as the chosen. Why would God pick such an objectionable, and at times repulsive, character? In other words, why does grace seek even the ungracious?

Week Five: Unlikely Choices

Focus readings: 27:5-10, 18-19, 41-44; 28:10-15, 20-21; 32:22-31; 33:1-10

OVERVIEW

God's choosing of Jacob represents an extraordinary risk taken in grace by selecting one so offensive to be the covenant's new promise-bearer. However, Jacob soon discovers that God's risk carries ramifications for his own life. Will he secure the promise by cunning and self-centered bargaining, or will he learn that the covenant's gifts depend upon trust? At story's end, reconciliation comes only after struggle—and a new recognition of where (and in whom) one sees the face of God.

How do these themes and issues relate to your faith community and the members of your study group? Some persons in the church may seem as morally unlikely as Jacob. How do others convey grace to those individuals? How do you? Some individuals and communities follow Jacob's example of self-made success at any cost. Where might the members of your group draw the line, say, in what they think the church should do in order to attract new members? Is any method or approach justified as long as it works? Finally, consider those among your group who may be struggling with the issue of reconciliation in family, among friends, even within the church. What does the Jacob narrative say to those individuals?

PREPARING FOR THE SESSION

Reflect on the stories of Jacob both in scripture and in the daily reading. Try to understand how persons in the group might hear these same stories this week. What might they hear differently from you? Where might these stories impact their lives? Pray for God's guidance in your preparation and leading.

Resources Needed

- (worship center) Large Bible opened to Genesis 33:10, construction paper of various colors, scissors, markers, tape or pins to fasten papers around the worship center
- Hymnals or songbooks with "Jacob's Ladder" and any musical accompaniment that someone can provide
- Blank unlined paper and pens

LEADING THE SESSION

Grace Calls Us

- Greet participants by name as they enter. Introduce any guests or newcomers to the others.
- Instruct each person to cut out the outline of a face from the construction paper (either a front view or silhouette). Encourage persons to picture the face of someone they care for to serve as the pattern. Assure persons that artistic skill is not the point of this activity. Persons may leave the face blank, or they may use markers to indicate eyes, nose, etc. Stress keeping such details to a minimum. As persons complete the cut-out, display them on or around the worship center so they are visible during the session.
- Distribute hymnals or songbooks and sing "Jacob's Ladder." Briefly discuss how the words and mood of that song relate to the stories read through this week.

ALTERNATE EXPERIENCE Tell participants to find a partner. Discuss contemporary parallels to God's unlikely choice of Jacob. For example, what persons or groups do members find troublesome or disagreeable while having a sense of God's working through them? Why might God make such choices?

- Offer this or a similar prayer of invocation: *Holy God, move among us in ways we do not anticipate—in thoughts that are new, in persons we didn't expect, in grace that catches us by surprise. Remind us that you are the God of Jacob as well as Abraham; the God who startles us in a manger, among sinners, and on a cross. In Jesus Christ. Amen.*

Grace Forms Us

• Distribute paper and pens. Instruct persons to fold the paper in half twice, forming four sections. Direct the participants' attention to the faces displayed by the worship center. Have each person silently choose one to represent the face of Jacob. Say aloud, "First, imagine what that face looked like when Jacob cheated Esau and lied to his father. In one quarter of the paper, write down what you see in Jacob's face. (*Clarify that persons could note physical characteristics or the emotions they 'read' in his face.*) Second, imagine what Jacob's face looked like the morning after his dream of the ladder. Write down what you see in that face in another quarter of the paper. Third, imagine what Jacob's face looked like while he wrestled the stranger at night. Write down what you see in another quarter of the paper. Fourth, imagine what Jacob's face looked like when he saw in Esau's face something of the face of God. Write that down in the last quarter." When everyone has finished, form groups of three or four persons to discuss the papers. Compare and contrast what persons saw. Move the discussion to more personal reflection, to times when their faces reflected what they saw in Jacob's face. How did God work through their times of deceit, bargaining, struggle, and reconciliation to bring grace?

ALTERNATE EXPERIENCE Do the above as a guided imagery exercise in place of writing. Invite persons to relax. Closed eyes and consciousness of one's breathing help set the context. Begin by offering words that place the members as unseen witnesses by Jacob's side at each of the significant times in his life. Take time to allow the participants to see what is in Jacob's eyes, how his forehead curls or smooths, and other such details with each encounter. At the end of the guided imagery experience, invite persons to share in small groups the faces— and changes—they saw. Discuss how their perceptions of Jacob's face derived from their own experiences of such times in their lives.

- After using either of the above experiences, discuss the transition Jacob makes from being one who relies on himself and his guile to achieve what he wants to being one who trusts in God. What are the highlights of those changes? What elements of the story's end suggest that the transformation of character might still be ongoing? How does Jacob's journey to trusting grace compare to our own?

- In pairs, discuss Jacob and Esau's reunion. How does this speak to our experiences and needs for reconciliation? What does it mean for us that Esau calls the one who cheated him "brother," that Jacob saw in Esau the face of God?

Grace Commissions Us

- Gather the group in the worship area. Summarize these (and/or other) main themes involved in the life of Jacob and God's gracious choice of him: forgiveness (*without it, Jacob could have been disenfranchised from the promise, and Esau might have taken vengeance*), tenacity (*God's steadfast relationship with Jacob, and Jacob's love for Rebekah*), renewal (*God eventually brings change and a new identity to Jacob*), and reconciliation (*reunion of brothers and Jacob's trusting of God's promises by returning*).

ALTERNATE EXPERIENCE Say, "Look again at the face in the worship center that you imagined earlier as the face of

Jacob. See it now as a mirror. Examine your own life in the light of Jacob's story: What shows on your face? In what ways are you still trying to control and manipulate for your benefit? Consider relationships: Where are you on the run from another or from yourself? In what areas of your life are you wrestling with God? Where are you experiencing the grace of seeing God in others? Wherever you are, Jacob's narrative affirms that God is there, waiting to be gracious, waiting for grace to be trusted.

"Focus on the face you drew, and recall the person it depicts. How do you see the face of God in that person? How does he or she convey grace to your life?"

• Lead the group in a closing prayer that offers a time of silence for persons to thank God for those in whom we are graced to see God's face and a time to thank God for choosing us with grace. Conclude with a call for us to be good stewards of the choice and grace God extends to us.

REVIEW / PREVIEW

Only one session remains. Consider reviewing all the previous sessions. What issues might need revisiting? What sorts of activities have worked best and bear working into the next session plan?

With Joseph, God's grace and providence come tightly woven together—yet the weave is not without danger of unraveling. Dreams take time and even more trust. Abraham and Isaac's earlier discovery of God's providing finds renewed emphasis in the one who now moves from favored to enslaved to restored...to restorer. All in good time, all in good grace.

Week Six: Irrepressible Providence

Focus readings: 37:3-8, 17-21; 40:9-14; 41:9-14, 25-41; 42:6-8; 45:1-5: 50:15-26

OVERVIEW

The closing stories in Genesis explore God's grace from a variety of perspectives: the waiting that providence evokes even when good seems to go unrewarded and unremembered; the consideration of how persons use the power entrusted to them, and how the recognition of the source of such power influences its exercise; the ability of grace to overturn convention (and attempts to manipulate it), receiving one final affirmation in Jacob's blessing of Joseph's sons.

Consider how such perspectives address the lives and issues of the persons in this study group and your faith community. Who waits for providence to reveal itself in the midst of trying times, and how does the church offer support? In what ways has the exercise of power brought forgiveness or further alienation in your congregation or wider community? How might persons in the study group relate to the way grace surprises us and eludes our efforts to "domesticate" it?

PREPARING FOR THE SESSION

Read the stories of Joseph with an eye to the ways in which grace speaks through his changing situations: from favored son, to falsely accused, to forgotten prisoner, to Pharaoh's advisor, to reconciler of brothers, to a seeker of his sons' blessing. With "which" Joseph might you and/or your study group members most identify; how might the experience of God's grace in that context of Joseph's life address your own?

Resources Needed
- (worship center) Cross, collage (completed in class)
- (collage) Magazines with pictures (variety is important), scissors, large sheet(s) of newsprint or poster board, glue or paste
- Lined paper, pens or pencils
- Hymnbooks that contain "Amazing Grace" and at least three of the following hymns: "O God of Earth and Space," "Give to the Winds Thy Fears," "If Thou But Trust in God to Guide Thee," "Guide Me, O Thou Great Jehovah," and/or other hymns about God's providence
- Evaluation form prepared by leader

LEADING THE SESSION

Grace Calls Us
- Welcome members to the final session in this series. Introduce guests to group members. Thank persons for participating in the study these past six weeks.
- Invite persons to gather in a circle near the worship center. Ask them to silently consider in their minds what providence means to them: What images come to mind? How does grace relate to providence? How do these stories from the past week relate to those ideas about providence and grace? Offer a brief prayer in thanksgiving for God's providence.
- Instruct persons to create a single collage that depicts aspects of God's providence, using pictures or single words cut from the magazines and pasted/glued to the sheet of newsprint or poster board. If the class is large, use several sheets but fasten them together to end up with a single collage. Allow time to create the collage. Post it at the worship center, as close to the cross as possible.

ALTERNATE EXPERIENCE Compare and contrast these visible images of providence with images found in hymns. Form groups of three or four and assign each group one of the hymns suggested above. Allow each group to report what their hymn reveals about the nature of providence. Ideally, sing one verse of each hymn to gain an idea how the melody or key influences the message.

Grace Forms Us

- Discuss the family dynamics portrayed in Genesis 37:1-11. Describe how each person or group (Joseph, Jacob, and the brothers) might justify their attitudes and relationship to the others. Ask everyone who is able to stand.

  Designate three corners or areas of the room (as Joseph, Jacob, and the brothers). Read Genesis 37:1-11 aloud. Based on this portion of the story alone, direct persons to stand in the area of the character with whom they most sympathize. Once participants have chosen, ask why they made those choices. Then ask each group where God is in relationship to that character(s). What is the reasoning behind that understanding?

- Invite participants to find a partner and review the story of Joseph and Potiphar's wife (39:1-23). Ask the partners to relate this episode to contemporary experience. Say, "In your own life, when has holding to your values or convictions resulted in a negative outcome? How do you know and/or judge when you can go along and compromise and when you cannot? How can loyalty or goodness be its own reward?

ALTERNATE EXPERIENCE Distribute paper and pens or pencils. Invite persons to place themselves in Joseph's position.

They are to write diary entries that relate personal feelings as well as reflections on their trust in God based on various experiences in Joseph's life. Ask them to consider each of the following experiences (*pause to give persons time to record the entry*):
—Two years after asking the cupbearer to remember you to Pharaoh, and you are still in prison (40:99-14, 20-23; 41:1).
—The evening after seeing your brothers for the first time since they sold you into slavery (42:6-24*a*).
—The morning of the day you realize you will die (50:24-26).

Afterward, ask members to find a partner and read their entries to each other. Discuss how the entries reflect their own experiences and faith.

- In the large group, discuss the roles played by power and forgiveness in this story. Who has power at various points in the narrative? How is it demonstrated? Who exercises forgiveness and why? Invite persons to draw parallels from these exercises of power and forgiveness in Joseph's time with our own. Imagine and discuss how these stories might play out in the arena of national politics: What if opponents forgave those who harmed them by saying, "Even though you intended to do me harm, God intended it for good"? Ask for a show of hands among group members as to which one of the following they would consider to be true of such an action: weakness, naivete, foolishness, graciousness.

- Imagine in silence how these stories might play out in the life of your congregation. Outside of the Sunday morning liturgy, are words of forgiveness frequently spoken?—for what? to whom? Where is forgiveness still needed? And how might we become instruments of grace that heal and reconcile? Allow persons an extended time of silent reflection to weigh these thoughts. If time permits, extend the

meditation to encompass families, and the grace and forgiveness needed there.

Grace Commissions Us

• Encourage persons to take seriously their thoughts on forgiveness in the context of your faith community. Invite them,
as an act of trust in the grace revealed in the Joseph stories, to
take some action that extends forgiveness—or encourages
those who are in need of its exercise or receiving.

ALTERNATE EXPERIENCE Remind group members of
the significant role that dreams play throughout the Joseph
story. Have participants call out the dreams that are part of our
lives: dreams for one's own life, for one's church, for one's family. Recall that what set apart Joseph as a dreamer before
Pharaoh was not simply his ability to interpret Pharaoh's dream
correctly, but his ability to develop plans that met the needs of
that dream. Looking back at the dreams mentioned by group
members, how do persons and the church build and plan to
make those dreams a reality? How do God's providence and
grace play a role in those plans and even the dreams themselves?

• Distribute evaluation forms and ask participants to take a
few minutes to fill them out and return them to you.

• Gather the group by the worship center. If possible, set the
collage directly alongside the cross. Invite group members
to look back over these past six sessions, to consider the
readings they have done in and about Genesis. Ask persons
to name what they have learned or rediscovered about grace.
Consider the collage and its images: How do providence
and grace interact in the story of Joseph? in the previous
stories of Genesis? in our own lives?

• Recall the closing story of this week's readings on Jacob's
cross-handed blessing. Grace surprises us because grace is

God's to give rather than ours to control. Close by asking members to keep that sense of grace as surprise alive, particularly as the events of Holy Week draw near. On the cross, God brings grace through the ultimate surprise of life won through death, of victory borne through suffering.
• Close by singing "Amazing Grace."

REVIEW / PREVIEW

For planning and leading future group studies, review the participants' evaluation forms. Pass these forms on to those responsible for planning such events in your congregation.

Thank you for the time and energy you have given to leading this study on Genesis!

About the Author

A native of St. Louis, JOHN INDERMARK now lives in the town of Naselle in southwest Washington with his wife, Judy, and son, Jeff. The author is an ordained minister in the United Church of Christ and has served U.C.C., United Methodist, and United Presbyterian congregations over the past twenty-one years. His published writing has included adult studies and other curriculm materials for *The Inviting Word* and *Bible Discovery*, as well as devotional articles for *The Upper Room Disciplines* (1997, 1998). When not involved in writing or parish work, you may find John flyfishing, beachcombing for agates, or watching Jeff play basketball.
